For Emma   Jan 1999

To learn and recite with Granny
when you come to visit.

Vanilla Gorilla

poems by
WILLIAM NEW

illustrated by
VIVIAN BEVIS

RONSDALE PRESS
1998

Vanilla Gorilla

A vanilla gorilla
      set off on a jog,
He ran to Toronto
      along with a frog,
A caramel camel
      got lost in the fog
With the king of the cereal boxes.

A skeleton followed
          and suddenly fell
In a beetle machine
          in a blackberry well,
The elegant elephant
          started to yell
At the king of the cereal boxes.

November Remember
          December and June,
The caribou left
          with a corduroy prune,
Now sing to yourself
          and a baby baboon
And the king of the cereal boxes.

My Uncle's Underwear

I dreamt I ate a guava
I dreamt I ate a pear
I dreamt I left Ungava
In my uncle's underwear

I dreamt I went to Java
I took a paddle there
I jumped upon the lava
In my uncle's underwear

I jumped upon the lava
'Cause both my feet were bare —
I didn't have an anorak
Or any boots to wear

Until I found a rubber tree
And climbed upon a chair
And picked a pair of rubberboots
A guava and a pear

And then I ate the guava
And then I ate the pear
And paddled to Ungava
In my uncle's underwear

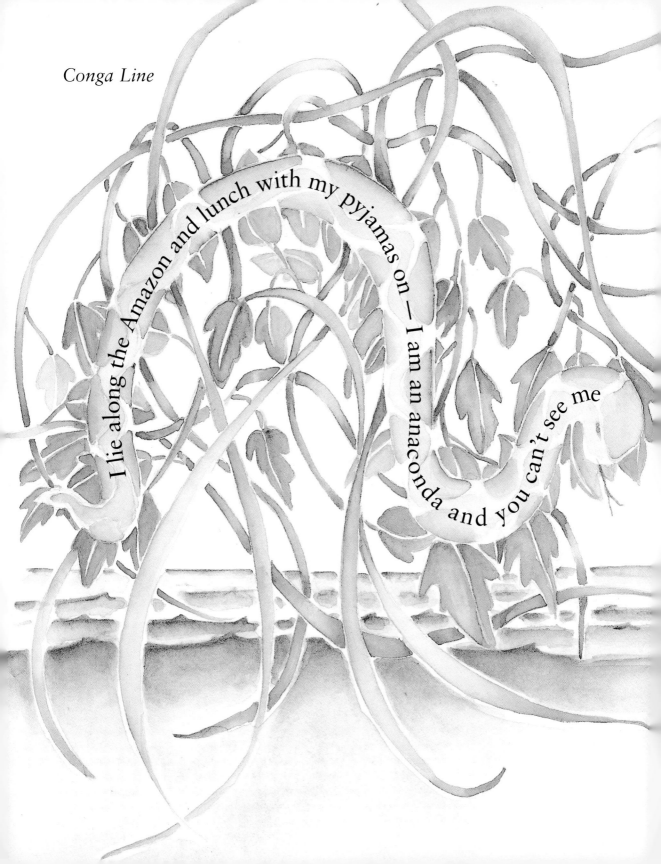

Conga Line

I lie along the Amazon and lunch with my pyjamas on — I am an anaconda and you can't see me

In Moose Jaw When It's Quiet

In Moose Jaw when it's quiet
And the Mountie's on a diet
And the only thing that's moving is the sun,
Make a meatball for your mother
Macaroni for your brother
And a muffin for your father, just for fun.

Antigonish the Fish

Said Antigonish the Fish
I wish   I wish   I wish
I could lie in the breeze
under barnacle trees
and eat with a fork and a dish.

My favourite hobby is food —
I'd eat Saskatoon if I could —
I'm especially fond
of fiddlehead frond
and fireweed honey and wood.

I'd gobble my fiddlehead meal
while driving an automobile —
and solving the puzzle
of learning to guzzle
with both of my fins at the wheel.

Then I'd lunch in Old Montreal
and crunch while I learned how to crawl
and even in Fogo
where old buffalo go
I'd munch while I grew to be tall.

As I can't get these morsels at sea,
on land is where I should be —
I'd like to relax
with the very best snacks
in a place where the meal won't be me.

Mackerel Mockery Pickerel Pike

Mackerel mockery pickerel pike
I rode a piano, my dad rode a bike
Together we pedalled from Prince Edward Island
Mackerel mockery pickerel pike

Pumpkin and pemmican, parkas and pine
Dad's getting purple but I'm feeling fine
We rode up to Parliament just to be prominent
Pickerel mackerel mockery mine

Ptarmigan tarragon tillicum tea
We rode in pyjamas to Sault Ste. Marie
We passed a pecan in a catamaran
Mockery pickerel mackerel me

Canteloupe antelope Alberta peach
We rode into Rockies and rode out of reach
We got to Vancouver in time for croquet
Mockery mackerel pickerel play

Polar-bear molars and meadows of mink
Upon the Pacific we started to sink:
I rowed the piano, my dad rowed the bike
Mackerel mockery pickerel pike

Being Only

In the land of Only Children
Where the Pirate Parents roar,
You must never lick the sugar cubes
That fall upon the floor —

And there's a lot of other things
They say you mustn't do:
You mustn't gargle with your milk,
Or hammer with your shoe —

It's even hard to breathe the air
Where Only Children dwell,
For someone always breathes it first
To test it for its smell:

There's always someone watching you
    To weigh how old you are,
        And measure up your manners
            In a silver samovar —

They tell you that you're bigger now,
Grow up and act your age —
But next they say you're little still,
And keep you in a cage —

I feel like hidden treasure
That is hoarded in a sieve —
It's really very hard to hide
Where Only Children live —

So if one day I have the chance
To be my opposite,
I'd like to live as triplets
Just to share the load a bit.

Inside Out

Shut the door! they always shout
whenever I go in or out,
It's cold in here! Keep out the flies!
You'll let in all the wasps! Surprise!
The summer stopped a month ago!
and other things like that. I know
that if I stopped to think I could
remember to be very good
with doors, but more important things —
like bubblegum and Saturn's rings
or fish and chips and chocolate pie
or playing basketball or why
the world is partly colourblind —
are usually upon my mind.

I think so hard my mind gets sore . . .
and then I forget to remember the door . . .

except last weekend I recall —
I just came back from playing ball
and closed the door when I walked inside —
I remember that: it was open wide —
Open the door! they shouted then —
The temperature's up to a hundred and ten!
Give us some air! and *Do not slam!*

Doors always get me in a jam.

Haiku

My grandmother laughs
with her eyes: Japanese
butterflies are less blue

*

When grandmother smiles
Japanese butterflies rise
to scatter the sky

By grandmother's eyes
wrinkles fan like butterflies:
Morning in Japan

*

Sleeping butterflies:
the eyes of my grandmother
rest like folded wings

Pandas

Who knows if
panda bears still
play when they're a-
lone
Who knows what
music plays when
pandas are at
home?

                In
      China a
      panda
      out on a verandah
      played upon a
      mandolin where
      linnets once sang
      long.

Who knows where
panda bears re-
main when they're a-
lone?
Who knows where a
panda goes when
people stay at
home?
                In
            China a
            panda
            rode upon a
            Honda
            gambolled down a
            mountainside where
            linnets once sang
            long.

Code Comfort

I've got a code, I say to Mum
                You've got a cold? you're feeling glum?
No, no, I say, You heard me wrong
                But Well, *she says,* Stick out your tongue!
You didn't hear me right, I say,
I've got a letter code today,
Just listen and pretend I'm Morse —
                That cold is bad. You say you're worse?
                You'd better go to bed at once
                Or you'll be sick for months and months.
No, my code's an alphabet —
                You're awful bad? Then off you get
                You go upstairs and get some rest
                I'll put some mustard on your chest —
Listen, Mum, you take some letters —
                Lots of people say they never
                Catch a cold, but when one comes
                They have to listen to their mums —

Then you substitute some others —
        Yes, they listen to their mothers —
The letters o-m-k-n-i-
        Oh you're aching in your eye?
Spell out a-j-p-m-y-
        Eh? It's hard to say just why —
The word 'kimono' spells 'pyjama' —
        Good, I'm glad you love your mama:
        Now what's the awful heavy sigh for?
Don't you see the secret cipher?
All my code is in my head!
        But all she says is: Off to bed!

When the Dinosaur Bones go Dancing

The dew worms rise to the DEW-line sky
    when the dinosaur bones go dancing.

The dew worms rise and the dogwoods sigh,
the dogwoods bloom and the days go dry
    when the dinosaur bones go dancing.

The dogwoods bloom where the moon rides high,
the moon men call and the bone men cry —
the dogwoods fall if there's no reply
    when the dinosaur bones go dancing.

Listen: watch for the moon man's eye,
Watch as the waterless moon comes nigh,
Watch and beware, the dogwoods sigh,
The bone men sing and the dew worms fly
    when the dinosaur bones go dancing.

Grandma Dances Anagrams

There's an ANT in ANTicosti
And a MASK in AkiMiSKi
There's an ACROBAT in FORt MACleod AlBerTa
There's a MAN in MANitoulin
And a PIG in WinnIPeG, and there's a
             DANCE in CumbErlAND
      when Grandma dances

There's a MISS in MISSissauga
And a BATH in AthaBATHsca
There's a KING who loves to SING in KapuskaSING
There's a EWE in NEW WEstminster
And a RAM in Crysler's FARM, and there's a
        DANCE in KiNCArDinE
        when Grandma dances

There's a CAN in the AtlANtiC
And a GIANT in MeGANTic
There's a BISON ON A VAN in BONAVIStA
There's a CART of ART in ARCTic
And a CRAB in HarBour GRACe, and there's a
        DANCE in DAwsoN CrEek
        when Grandma dances

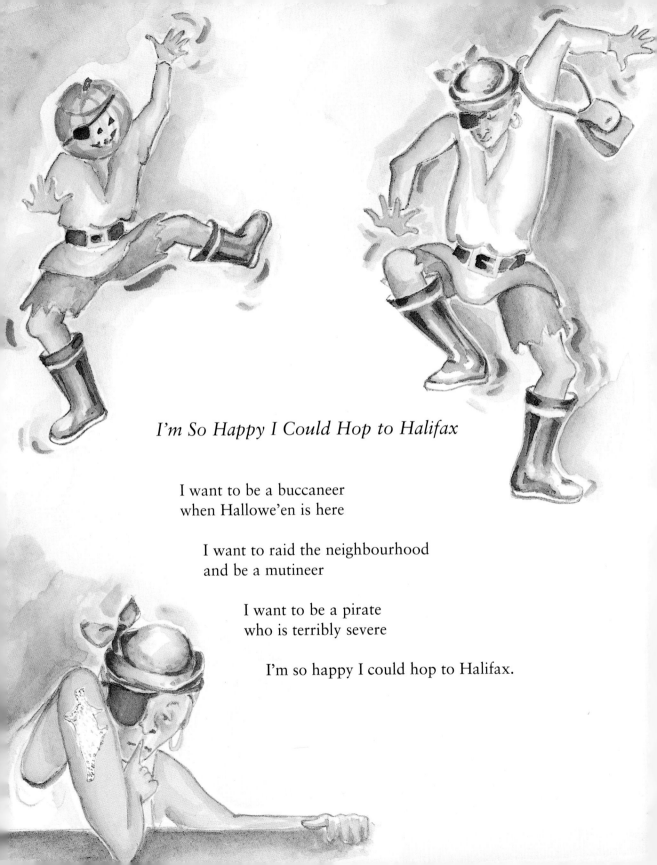

I'm So Happy I Could Hop to Halifax

I want to be a buccaneer
when Hallowe'en is here

I want to raid the neighbourhood
and be a mutineer

I want to be a pirate
who is terribly severe

I'm so happy I could hop to Halifax.

I want to fly the skull and bones
and be a bugaboo

I want to be a pirate
with a terrible tattoo

I want a case of candybars
when Hallowe'en is through

I'm so happy I could hop to Halifax.

My Narwhal is a Nincompoop

My narwhal is a nincompoop
He's nosy and he nags
He wears a neon necklace
And he punctures paper bags
    He tries to swim to Pangnirtung
    Every New Year's Day
    But ends up down in Newfoundland
    Instead of Baffin Bay

My narwhal is a nincompoop
He's nervous as a gnat
Whenever he goes out to sea
He natters through his hat
      He swims about the neighbourhood
      At nearly ninety knots
      And when he gets to Newfoundland
      He nibbles apricots

My narwhal is a nincompoop
He's noisy when he sings
He cannot nicely nuzzle you
Because he always stings
      He hasn't got a nickname
      He needs a Needle-friend
      And if you come from Newfoundland
      You'll know that he's

THE END

VANILLA GORILLA
Text Copyright © 1998 William New
Illustrations Copyright © 1998 Vivian Bevis

RONSDALE PRESS
3350 West 21st Avenue
Vancouver, B.C. Canada V6S 1G7
www.ronsdalepress.com

Typesetting: Julie Cochrane, Vancouver, BC
Printing: Printcrafters, Winnipeg, Manitoba

The publisher acknowledges the financial support of the Canada Council for the Arts,
the Government of Canada through the Book Publishing Industry Development Program, and
the British Columbia Cultural Services Branch for our publishing activities.

CANADIAN CATALOGUING IN PUBLICATION DATA
New, W.H. (William Herbert), 1938–
Vanilla Gorilla

ISBN 0-921870-57-4

I. Bevis, Vivian, (date)   II. Title.
PS8577.E776V36 1998   jC811'.54   C98-910194-0
PZ7.N4655Va 1998

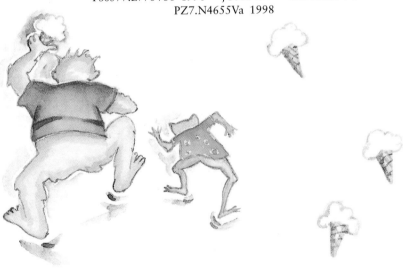